LAUREL BURCH
LEGENDS

C&T PUBLISHING

Text and Artwork © 2007 C&T Publishing

Artwork: © 2007 Laurel Burch

Publisher: Amy Marson

Editorial Director: Gailen Runge

Developmental Editors: Cyndy Lyle Rymer and Darra Williamson

Technical Editors: Rene J. Steinpress and Joyce E. Lytle

Copyeditor/Proofreader: Wordfirm Inc.

Design Director/Cover & Book Designer: Christina D. Jarumay

Illustrators: Mary Ann Tenorio and Kirstie Pettersen

Production Coordinator: Tim Manibusan

Photography: Luke Mulks and Diane Pedersen unless otherwise noted. Author photo by Laurel Burch Studio.

Published by: C&T Publishing, Inc., P.O. Box 1456, Lafayette, CA 94549

Front Cover: *Sea Goddess* by Patricia Morris

Back Cover: *Swan Goddess* by Cyndy Lyle Rymer, and *Spirits of the Sky* by Sue Mead

Library of Congress Cataloging-in-Publication Data

Burch, Laurel.

  Laurel Burch legends. 9 quilts inspired by the earth, sea & sky / Laurel Burch.

    p. cm.

  Includes bibliographical references.

  ISBN-13: 978-1-57120-367-0 (paper trade : alk. paper)

  ISBN-10: 1-57120-367-2 (paper trade : alk. paper)

  1. Patchwork--Patterns. 2. Machine appliqué--Patterns. 3. Machine quilting. 4. Nature in art. I. Title. II. Title: 9 quilts inspired by the earth, sea & sky.

TT835.B8173 2007

746.46'041--dc22

                          2006026712

Printed in China

10 9 8 7 6 5 4 3 2 1

DEDICATION

To my loving family –

my husband, Rick;

my daughter, Aarin;

my son, Juaquim; and my grand-

daughters, Karly and Soffiya

EDITORS' ACKNOWLEDGMENTS

The editors wish to thank the following for their generosity and talent:

The Warm Company, for Warm & Natural batting

Golden Threads, for their wonderful Quilting Paper

RJR Fabrics, Hoffman California Fabrics, and Blank Textiles (and their employees), for providing fabric to make the quilts

The fabulous quiltmakers, Helen Frost, Sophie Littlefield, Barbara K. Baker, Cyndy Lyle Rymer, Sue Mead, and Patricia Morris, for the investment of time and the meticulous workmanship that resulted in the projects you see in these pages

Finally—and most of all—we are grateful to Laurel Burch, one of the most charismatic and talented artists we have had the pleasure to work with!

Contents

welcome to the world of my imagination!

I want to capture the brilliant, rainbow colors of the world, its creatures, its people... with designs that remind us of our connectedness to one another... creating symbols that bridge the gap between ages, races, cultures and beliefs, and even the physical and spiritual worlds.

As an artist, I am deeply committed to the purpose of brightening lives and lifting spirits, and I am grateful for the many kindred souls I have found through my art who share my art and dreams with me.

Blessings to All!

Laurel

PAJAROS

Pajaros

15½˝ × 11˝, hand appliquéd, embellished, and machine quilted by Helen Frost, Tucson, AZ, 2006.

MATERIALS

Read through Tips and Techniques for Appliqué and Embellishment (page 50) before beginning this or any project. Refer to that chapter as needed throughout construction. Yardages are based on fabrics with a usable width of 40˝.

- **Light blue:** ½ yard for background

- **Dark blue and magenta:** ⅓ yard *each* for birds

- **Purple, red, and gold:** ¼ yard *each* for birds

- **Orange:** ⅛ yard for beaks

- **White, brown, and royal blue:** Small scraps of *each* for eyes

- **Acid green:** ⅛ yard for leaves and birds

- **Olive green and kelly green:** ¼ yard *each* for leaves

- **Black:** ¼ yard for bird details and binding

- **Backing:** 20˝ × 15˝

- **Batting:** 20˝ × 15˝ piece

- **Thread:** Cotton or silk thread to match the appliqués and gold metallic for quilting

- **Fabric paints:** Pale blue and aquamarine

- **Fabric pen:** Black brush-point and gold metallic

- **Sequins:** Three 8mm gold

- **Glass beads:** 3 gold

tip

Since acute inside angles can be difficult to hand appliqué, disguise them instead. Paint the inside of the angle to match the background fabric. Turn and stitch only the outer edge of the piece.

CUTTING

Cut all strips across the width of the fabric (selvage to selvage).

- **From the light blue:**
  Cut 1 rectangle 19˝ × 15˝.*

- **From the black:**
  Cut 2 strips 2˝ × 40˝.

* This piece is cut oversized; you will trim it after the appliqué is complete.

MAKING PAJAROS

Note: Helen hand appliquéd this project, and the instructions are written for that method, but you can adapt the instructions as needed and machine appliqué if you wish. Refer to the photos throughout the project for inspiration and ideas for embellishment.

1. Enlarge the pattern on page 11 as directed. Center and transfer the pattern to the 19˝ × 15˝ piece of light blue fabric.

2. Prepare the templates for cutting the appliqués. Cut out the appliqué pieces, adding a ³⁄₁₆˝ seam allowance. Do not cut or clip the V-shaped breaks in the leaves.

3. Cover your work surface to protect it for painting.

4. Use the fabric paint to paint the V-shaped breaks in the sides of the leaves to match the background they will be placed on. See the tip and detail below for guidance.

Detail of painting on leaves

5. Use the black and gold pens to draw details on the appliqué pieces, such as the veins on the leaves, the birds' beaks, and the stripes on the birds' top feathers.

6. Heat set the paints and inks according to the manufacturer's instructions.

7. Position and hand stitch the appliqué pieces to the marked background fabric.

8. Trim the appliquéd piece to 15½″ × 11″.

FINISHING THE QUILT

1. Layer the quilt top, batting, and backing. Pin or thread baste the layers together.

2. Use gold metallic thread to quilt around the leaves and birds. Quilt the center vein on the larger leaves and along the head and eye pieces on the birds.

3. Anchor a gold sequin with a gold bead to create an eye for each bird.

4. Trim and square the quilt as necessary. Use the 2″ × 40″ black strips to bind the quilt, using your preferred method.

⑥ Home, Sweet Home

The size and shape of *Pajaros* make it perfect for adaptation as a pillow. A book such as *Pillows: 29 Projects for Stylish Living* by Jean and Valori Wells can give you the basic information you need to accomplish this, including instructions for making an appropriately sized pillow insert (see Resources and Bibliography on page 61). Add piping or other decorative elements to enhance the design.

Detail of bird's embellished eye

Enlarge 180%

Celestial Birds

15½″ × 16″, machine appliquéd, embellished, and machine quilted by Sophie Littlefield, Danville, CA, 2006. Fabric generously provided by RJR Fabrics.

MATERIALS

Read through Tips and Techniques for Appliqué and Embellishment (page 50) before beginning this or any project. Refer to that chapter as needed throughout construction. Yardages are based on fabrics with a usable width of 40˝.

- **Mottled red:** ⅝ yard for background and backing
- **Deep royal blue:** ¼ yard for waves and binding
- **Light blue, fuchsia, light and dark purple, reddish purple, orange, and yellow-gold:** Scraps of *each* for birds, waves, and sun
- **Batting:** 20˝ × 20˝ piece
- **Fusible web:** 1 yard
- **Tear-away stabilizer:** 1 yard
- **Thread:** Red, dark purple, royal blue, light blue, yellow variegated, and fuchsia rayon, and gold metallic to match the appliqués for satin stitching, quilting, and other decorative stitching
- **Fabric paint:** Gold metallic, green metallic, silver metallic, white, blue, pink, orange, and light purple
- **Marking tool:** Mechanical pencil or water-soluble marker
- **Fabric marker:** Black

Detail of large bird's wing and waves

CUTTING

Cut all strips across the width of the fabric (selvage to selvage).

- **From the mottled red:**

  Cut 1 rectangle 17½˝ × 18˝.

  Cut 1 square 20˝ × 20˝.

- **From the deep royal blue:**

  Cut 2 strips 2˝ × 40˝; set the remaining fabric aside for appliqués.

MAKING CELESTIAL BIRDS

Refer to the photos throughout the project for inspiration and ideas for embellishment.

1. Enlarge the pattern on page 15 as directed. Center and transfer the pattern to the 17½˝ × 18˝ piece of mottled red fabric.

2. Prepare the templates for cutting the appliqués. Cut out all the appliqué shapes.

3. Cover your work surface to protect it for painting.

4. Mix the blue and white paints to make light blue, and then paint the triangle shapes for the 2 largest bird tails using the light blue, orange, and pink paint. Paint triangles directly on the smallest bird's tail with light blue and light purple paint. Paint triangles on each bird's upper wings with 2 contrasting colors.

5. Paint the white of each bird's eye. Let dry, and then dot each with the black fabric marker to create the iris. Once the eyes are dry, outline each eye with the black fabric marker.

6. Paint the lower edge of each light blue wing shape with green metallic paint. Add accents with gold metallic paint to the top of each bird's head.

7. Accent some of the wave shapes with silver metallic paint.

8. Paint gold metallic highlights on the left and right sides of the sun.

9. Heat set the paints and inks according to the manufacturer's instructions.

10. Use a mechanical pencil or water-soluble marker and a light touch to sketch the feather design on the piece for each bird.

11. Back the entire quilt top with tear-away stabilizer. Position and pin or baste all the appliqué shapes to the marked background piece. For the birds, layer the upper wing pieces, the light blue wing pieces, the tails, and then the lower wing pieces. Finally, add the body shapes and beaks. Fuse all the pieces in place.

12. Use a satin stitch and the various colored threads to appliqué the shapes in place, varying the stitch width to achieve the desired effects. Remove the tear-away stabilizer.

Detail of medium bird

FINISHING THE QUILT

1. Layer the quilt top, batting, and backing. Pin or thread baste the layers together.

2. Stitch in-the-ditch around all the major appliqué shapes. Use gold metallic thread to stitch the marked feather designs on the wing of each bird. Stitch a line down each bird's beak. Use matching or contrasting thread to outline the triangle designs on the birds' tails and wings. Stipple quilt a circle design on each bird's body. Outline quilt several circles radiating from the sun in gold metallic thread. Outline quilt the remainder of the background in red thread.

3. Trim and square the quilt to 15½″ × 16″. Use the 2″ × 40″ deep royal blue strips to bind the quilt, using your preferred method.

Enlarge 240%

Earth Mother

53½″ × 18½″, machine appliquéd, pieced, and quilted by Barbara K. Baker, Bend, OR, 2006. Fabrics generously provided by Hoffman California Fabrics.

MATERIALS

Read through Tips and Techniques for Appliqué and Embellishment (page 50) before beginning this or any project. Refer to that chapter as needed throughout construction. Yardages are based on fabrics with a usable width of 40˝.

- **Muslin:** 1⅝ yards for foundation
- **Skin tone:** Fat quarter for woman's face
- **Dark blue:** ½ yard for sky
- **2 light blues, 3 or 4 medium blues, 2 dark blues, and 1 multicolored blue:** Large scraps (up to 40˝ long) of *each* for hair and bird
- **Light yellow:** Fat quarter for moon and sun
- **Medium yellow:** Fat quarter for sun and flowers
- **Fuchsia, 3 or 4 purples, 2 or 3 pinks, 2 oranges, 2 reds/pinks, blue, and white:** Fat quarter *each* or scraps for sun, flowers, bird, and eyes
- **Light green, medium green, and dark green:** Fat quarter *each* for leaves and bird
- **Black:** 2 yards for binding and backing
- **Batting:** 58˝ × 23˝ piece
- **Fusible web:** 5 yards
- **Thread:** Invisible thread for appliqué and quilting, lightweight bobbin thread, and decorative thread (optional) for binding
- **Fabric paints:** Black, metallic gold, blue, pink, red, white, purple, yellow, and green
- **Small paintbrush and metal-tip paint applicator**
- **Specialty rotary blade** (optional) for cutting scalloped, fused binding strips

CUTTING

- **From the muslin:**

  Cut 1 rectangle 55˝ × 21˝.*

- **From the black fabric:**

  Cut 1 rectangle 58˝ × 23˝.

  Cut 1 strip 8½˝ × 56˝.

* This piece is cut oversized; you will trim it after the appliqué is complete.

Detail of flowers and leaves

MAKING EARTH MOTHER

Refer to the photos throughout the project for inspiration and ideas for embellishment. The full-sized pattern for *Earth Mother* is on pullout 1 at the back of the book. Note that the pattern comprises both sides of this pullout.

1. Center and transfer the full-sized *Earth Mother* pattern to the 55″ × 21″ rectangle of muslin fabric.

2. Prepare the templates for cutting the appliqués. Cut out all the appliqué shapes.

3. Cover your work surface to protect it for painting.

4. Use the various colors of fabric paint to add interior details to the woman's face, bird, flowers, leaves, moon, and sun. Do not outline the pieces or add dots to the sky or the woman's hair yet.

5. Position and pin or baste all the appliqué shapes to the marked muslin piece. Fuse all the pieces in place.

6. Use a straight stitch and invisible thread to appliqué the shapes in place. If you elect to use a satin stitch to appliqué the shapes, consider using tear-away stabilizer (see Stitching on page 54).

7. Outline all the appliqué shapes with black or gold metallic paint. Add paint dots of various colors to the woman's hair and the sky.

8. Heat set the paints and inks according to the manufacturer's instructions.

9. Trim the appliquéd piece to 53½″ × 18½″.

FINISHING THE QUILT

The quilt shown was finished with a fusible binding that Barbara trimmed with a specialty rotary blade to add a decorative edge to the quilt top. You can duplicate this technique following the instructions below, or cut 2″-wide strips from the black fabric and bind as desired.

1. Layer the quilt top, batting, and backing. Pin or thread baste the layers together.

2. Quilt as desired with invisible thread. Trim the batting and backing even with the quilt top.

3. Cut an 8½″ × 56″ strip from the remaining fusible web. Follow the manufacturer's instructions to fuse the web to the back of the 8½″ × 56″ black strip. From this larger strip, cut 2 strips 2″ × 21″ and 2 strips 2″ × 55″, using a specialty rotary blade if desired.

Cut narrow strips from the prepared fabric with a specialty blade.

4. Fold the binding in half, fabric side out, along the long edge; finger-press or use a wooden pressing tool.

Finger-press or use a wooden pressing tool to crease the binding strips.

5. Remove the paper backing from the fused fabric strips. Center and place one 2″ × 55″ binding strip over the top edge of the quilt, lining up the crease with the quilt edge. Fuse the binding to the front of the quilt. Turn the quilt over and fold the binding strip to the back of the quilt. Fuse the strip to the back. Trim the excess binding even with the side edges of the quilt. Repeat to fuse a 2″ × 55″ binding strip to the bottom edge of the quilt.

Use the crease to position the fused binding.

6. Lightly fuse the 2″ × 21″ side binding strips to the front of the quilt. Wrap the excess binding fabric to the back. Cut and place a small piece of fusible web under each folded corner and fuse the side binding strips to the back of the quilt.

Secure the corners with small pieces of fusible web.

7. Topstitch the binding in place with invisible or decorative thread.

Detail of woman and bird

Folkloric Fish

13″ × 36″, machine appliquéd by
Cyndy Lyle Rymer, Danville, CA,
2006. Fabric generously provided
by Blank Textiles.

MATERIALS

Read through Tips and Techniques for Appliqué and Embellishment (page 50) before beginning this or any project. Refer to that chapter as needed throughout construction. Yardages are based on fabrics with a usable width of 40″.

- **Blue-green:** 1⅛ yards for background and backing

- **Purple, red, orange, yellow, yellow-orange, blue, lime green, medium green, and aqua:** Scraps of *each* for fish

- **Heavyweight fast2fuse interfacing:** 2 yards*

- **Freezer paper**

- **Thread:** Gold metallic for satin stitch and blue-green or contrasting color for finishing edges

- **Fabric paint:** White

- **Fabric markers:** Gold metallic, black, and green

- **Chunky pencil** with large eraser

- **Nonstick (Teflon) pressing sheet**

- **Steam-A-Seam tape:** ½″ wide

* See Resources and Bibliography on page 61.

Detail of *Folkloric Fish*.

CUTTING

- From the blue-green fabric:

  Cut 1 rectangle 15″ × 38″.

  Cut 1 rectangle 13″ × 36″.

- From the heavyweight fast2fuse interfacing:

  Cut 1 rectangle 13″ × 36″.

MAKING FOLKLORIC FISH

Refer to the photos throughout the project for inspiration and ideas for embellishment. For this project, you will make templates from freezer paper.

1. Enlarge the fish patterns on pages 25–27 as directed.

2. Trace each fish (including all pieces) onto the paper (dull) side of the freezer paper. Cut out each fish as a single piece on the traced line.

Trace fish onto freezer paper.

3. Place each freezer-paper template paper (dull) side up on the fast2fuse interfacing. Trace each shape onto the interfacing and cut out each fish shape on the traced line.

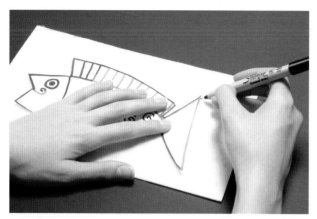

Trace freezer-paper template onto fast2fuse.

4. Working on one fish at a time, cut the freezer-paper templates apart to prepare for cutting the fabric for the individual fish sections, such as the fins and faces.

5. Press each freezer-paper template to the right side of the selected fabric. Cut out each shape approximately ⅛″ beyond the template.

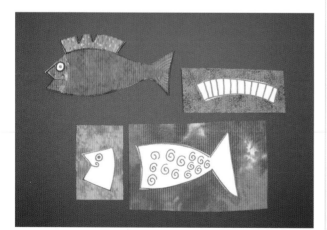

Press freezer-paper templates onto fabrics.

6. Cover your work surface to protect it for painting.

7. Create eyes on each fish face by lightly dipping the eraser of a chunky pencil into a dollop of white fabric paint and stamping it onto the fabric. If you would like an eye larger than the diameter of the eraser, gently widen the imprint by moving the eraser in small concentric circles. Let the paint dry completely.

8. Use the gold metallic, black, and green fabric markers to add details to the fish.

9. Heat set the paints and inks according to the manufacturer's instructions.

10. Working on one fish at a time, place all the painted and marked fabric pieces right side up on the matching fast2fuse fish shape. Place the entire unit on top of a nonstick pressing sheet and follow the manufacturer's instructions to fuse the pieces to the fast2fuse with a hot, dry iron. (The pressing sheet will prevent the fast2fuse from adhering to your ironing board cover.) When the fish are cool, turn them over and trim any excess fabric.

Trim excess fabric.

11. Place the 15″ × 38″ blue-green fabric rectangle right side down on your ironing board, and center the 13″ × 36″ rectangle of fast2fuse on top. Center the 13″ × 36″ blue-green (backing) rectangle fabric right side up on top of the fast2fuse. Working from the center and pressing *firmly* with the iron, fuse the backing fabric to the back of the fast2fuse. Turn the quilt sandwich over and press firmly to fuse the background fabric to the front of the fast2fuse.

12. Wrap the excess blue-green front fabric over the side edges to the back. Following the manufacturer's instructions, fuse a strip of Steam-A-Seam to the wrong side of the excess background fabric in preparation for fusing it to the back of the quilt. Fuse the excess fabric in place. Repeat for the top and bottom edges.

13. Working from the front, topstitch ¼″ from the edge all around the quilt perimeter.

14. Referring to the photo on page 20 and the layout diagram at right for fish placement, pin the "bottom layer" of fish onto the background. Use a zigzag stitch, satin stitch, or blanket stitch to sew the fish to the background. Add the rest of the overlapping fish one by one and stitch in the same manner.

tip

Fast2fuse is much stiffer than quilt batting. If you roll and fasten the edges of the quilt with a clothespin, binder clip, or other fastener, it will be easier to maneuver the piece in your sewing machine.

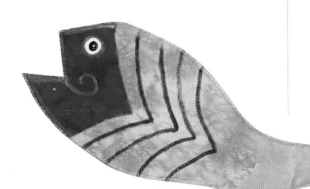

Home, Sweet Home

These fabulous fish can be used to make a number of other accessories for home decor or gift items. Instead of stitching the fish to a quilt as described in Making Folkloric Fish, Step 14, try one of the following options:

- Fuse each fish to a backing fabric in a complementary color and/or print, inserting a 12″–18″ length of ribbon or nylon fishing line into the top edge. Tie the opposite edge of the ribbon or line to a painted or covered dowel to create a colorful mobile.

- Fuse each smaller-sized fish to a backing fabric in a complementary color and/or print, inserting a 3″ loop of ⅛″- or ¼″-wide ribbon into the top edge…perfect for placing on your holiday tree.

- Fuse a smaller-sized fish to a backing fabric in a complementary color and/or print, inserting ribbon or cording into the top edge. Use the fish as a whimsical fan or shade pull or as a doorknob decoration.

Layout diagram

Enlarge 200%

Enlarge 200%

Enlarge 200%

Spirits of the Sky
Table Runner

59½˝ × 14½˝, machine appliquéd and quilted by Sue Mead, Dublin, CA, 2006.

MATERIALS

Read through Tips and Techniques for Appliqué and Embellishment (page 50) before beginning this or any project. Refer to that chapter as needed throughout construction. Yardages are based on fabrics with a usable width of 40˝.

- **Light yellow:** 1¾ yards for background and backing

- **Violet, purple, fuchsia, light pink, yellow, light green, orange, pink-orange, green, and aqua:** Scraps of *each* for birds, butterflies, dragonflies, flowers, and leaves

- **Batting:** 64˝ × 18˝ piece

- **Fusible web:** 1 yard

- **Tear-away stabilizer:** 1 yard

- **Thread:** Gold metallic and colors to match appliqués for satin stitch and other decorative stitching, and invisible nylon thread for quilting

- **Fabric markers:** Green, black, red, orange, and gold metallic

- **Multicolored ¼˝-wide pastel ribbon:** 4 yards

- **Steam-A-Seam tape:** ¼˝-wide

CUTTING

- **From the light yellow:**

  Cut 2 rectangles 15˝ × 60˝.

MAKING SPIRITS OF THE SKY

For this project, the birds, dragonflies, flowers, and leaves in combination are made separately and satin stitched and embellished before being fused to the background. The runner is finished in envelope style, so no binding is required. Refer to the photos throughtout the project for inspiration and ideas for embellishment.

1. Enlarge the patterns on pages 32–33 as directed.

2. Prepare the templates for cutting the appliqués. Cut out all the appliqué shapes.

Detail of angled runner end

3. Pin or thread baste a piece of tear-away stabilizer to the back of each appliqué piece before you begin stitching. Use the gold metallic and matching threads to satin stitch the raw edges of each shape. Stitch both the interior and exterior raw edges. You will straight stitch the outer edges of the appliqués to the table runner after the top is layered with the batting and backing.

4. Use the fabric markers to add details such as veins on leaves, dots or spokes in the centers of the flowers, spirals on the dragonfly wings, the birds' eyes, and so on. Heat set the details with a dry iron.

5. Remove the stabilizer from the back of each appliqué shape. Apply the fusible web to prepare each shape for machine appliqué following the manufacturer's instructions. Set the appliqués aside.

6. Fold one 60″ × 15″ rectangle of light yellow fabric in half lengthwise to measure 60″ × 7½″. Align the 45° mark of your ruler on the fold and trim both ends to form points.

7. Building from the bottom up, position the appliqué shapes on the table runner top, referring to the table runner photo on page 28 for placement. For example, place the leaves first, then the flowers, and so on. Fuse all the pieces in place. To further secure the appliqués, stitch in-the-ditch at the inside of the satin stitching to secure all the flowers, birds, dragonflies, and leaves to the table runner.

8. Trim the batting to 60″ × 15″. On a clean, flat surface, layer the batting, then the runner top right side up, and then the remaining 60″ × 15″ light yellow rectangle right side down on top of the runner top. Trim the batting and backing ends to the same 45° angle as the table runner top. Pin or thread baste the layers together.

9. Sew all 3 layers together on the outside edge with a ¼″ seam, leaving a 6″ opening for turning. Turn the runner right side out so the batting is in the center of the sandwich. Press around the edges and hand stitch the opening closed with invisible stitches and matching thread.

10. Use invisible or decorative thread to echo quilt around all the appliqué shapes, if desired, and free-motion stitch clouds or larger flowers in the background.

11. Follow the manufacturer's instructions to fuse strips of ¼″-wide fusible tape to the back of the multicolored ribbon. Fuse the ribbon in place approximately ¼″ from the edge all around the table runner, angling the ribbon with a fold at each corner. Secure by stitching down the center of the ribbon with a favorite decorative stitch.

Home, Sweet Home

Choose a favorite motif from the table runner—for example, a hummingbird or dragonfly—to make a set of matching placements. Finish the ensemble by making napkins: simply serge the edges of 18″ squares cut from complementary fabric.

Detail of *Spirits of the Sky*

Enlarge 165%

Enlarge 165%

Kindred Spirits
of the Jungle

19″ × 27³⁄₈″, machine appliquéd, pieced, and quilted by Barbara K. Baker, Bend, OR, 2006.
Fabrics generously provided by Blank Textiles.

MATERIALS

Read through Tips and Techniques for Appliqué and Embellishment (page 50) before beginning this or any project. Refer to that chapter as needed throughout construction. Yardages are based on fabrics with a usable width of 40˝.

- **Skin tone:** Fat quarter for women's faces and body
- **White:** ½ yard for elephant and lamb
- **Black:** 1 yard for background and binding
- **Yellow:** ½ yard for background, cheetah, and flowers
- **Yellow-orange and purple:** Fat quarter *each* for background
- **Light green, medium green, and dark green:** Fat quarter or scraps of *each* for leaves
- **Assorted light and dark purples, fuchsias, pinks, reds, oranges, and blues:** Fat quarters or scraps of *each* for flowers and birds
- **Brown:** Scrap for hair
- **Backing:** 1 yard
- **Batting:** 24˝ × 32˝ piece
- **Fusible web:** 4 yards
- **Steam-A-Seam tape:** ¼˝-wide (optional)
- **Thread:** Invisible thread for appliqué and quilting, lightweight bobbin thread, and decorative thread (optional) for binding
- **Fabric paints:** Black, gold metallic, blue, pink, purple, green, white, red, and yellow
- **Small paintbrush and fine metal-tip paint applicator**

CUTTING

- **From the black:**

  Cut 1 rectangle 6½˝ × 30½˝.

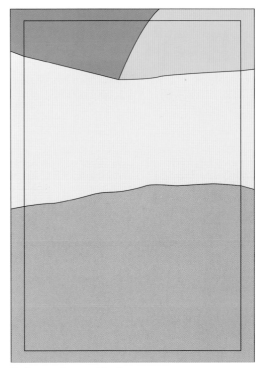

MAKING KINDRED SPIRITS OF THE JUNGLE

Refer to the photos throughout the project for inspiration and ideas for embellishment. The full-sized pattern for *Kindred Spirits* is on pullout 2 at the back of the book.

1. Refer to the background assembly diagram below and use the yellow, black, yellow-orange, and purple fabrics to prepare the background pieces. Add a ¼˝ seam allowance to all the pieces. Using the pattern pieces as a guide, cut a ¼˝-wide strip of fusible web (or use ¼˝-wide Steam-A-Seam tape) and fuse the pieces together. Lightly mark the borders for fabric placement guidelines.

Background assembly diagram
Add ¼˝ seam allowance to pattern pieces to allow for fusing.

2. Center and transfer the full-sized *Kindred Spirits* pattern to the prepared background piece. Set the background aside for now.

3. Prepare the templates for cutting the appliqués.

4. Cover your work surface to protect it for painting.

5. Use the various colors of paint to sponge paint the elephant fabric. Use the elephant template to fussy cut the elephant shapes after painting.

6. Cut out all the remaining appliqué shapes.

7. Use the various colors of fabric paint to add interior details to the women's faces, birds, animals, insects, flowers, and leaves. Do not outline the pieces or add details to the background yet.

8. Position and pin or baste all the appliqué shapes to the marked background. Fuse all the pieces in place. If you elect to use a satin stitch to appliqué the shapes, consider using tear-away stabilizer (see Stitching on page 54).

9. Outline all the appliqué shapes with black or gold metallic paint. Add paint dots of various colors to the background.

Use a fine metal-tip applicator with the fabric paints for accurate, finely drawn details.

10. Heat set the paints according to the manufacturer's instructions.

11. Trim the appliquéd piece to 19″ × 27⅜″.

FINISHING THE QUILT

The quilt shown was finished with a fusible binding that Barbara trimmed with a specialty rotary blade to add a decorative edge to the quilt top. You can duplicate this technique following the instructions below. Refer to *Earth Mother*, Finishing the Quilt (page 18), for additional guidance. If you prefer, cut 2″-wide strips from the black fabric and bind as desired.

1. Layer the quilt top, batting, and backing. Pin or thread baste the layers together.

2. Quilt as desired with invisible thread. Trim the batting and backing even with the quilt top.

3. Cut a 6½″ × 30½″ rectangle from the remaining fusible web. Follow the manufacturer's instructions to fuse the web to the back of the 6½″ × 30½″ black rectangle. From this rectangle, cut 2 strips 1½″ × 22″ and 2 strips 1½″ × 30½″, using a specialty rotary blade if desired.

tip

Some appliqués sit on top of the fused binding. Use sharp scissors to cut around the overhanging shapes. Slide the binding underneath, add fusible web to the underside of the overhanging pieces, and fuse.

Some appliqués overlap the binding.

4. Fold the binding in half along the long edge; finger-press or use a wooden pressing tool.

5. Remove the paper backing from the fused fabric strips. Center and place one 1½″ × 22″ binding strip over the top edge of the quilt, lining up the crease with the quilt edge. Fuse the binding to the front of the quilt. Turn the quilt over, folding the binding strip to the back of the quilt. Fuse the strip to the back. Trim the excess binding even with the side edges of the quilt. Repeat to fuse a 1½″ × 22″ binding strip to the bottom edge of the quilt.

6. Lightly fuse the 1½″ × 30½″ side binding strips to the front of the quilt. Fold the excess binding fabric to the back. Cut and place a small piece of fusible web under each folded corner and fuse the side binding strips to the back of the quilt.

7. Topstitch the binding in place with invisible or decorative thread.

Detail of woman holding the cheetah

Detail of sponge-painted elephant

Sea Goddess

19½″ × 22½″, machine appliquéd and quilted by Patricia Morris, Tucson, AZ, 2006.
Fabric generously provided by Hoffman California Fabrics.

MATERIALS

Read through Tips and Techniques for Appliqué and Embellishment (page 50) before beginning this or any project. Refer to that chapter as needed throughout construction. Yardages are based on fabrics with a usable width of 40˝.

- **Navy:** 1⅝ yards for background, backing, and binding

- **Blue:** ¼ yard *each* of 4 different blues for waves

- **Speckled blue:** ¼ yard for waves

- **Lime green, medium speckled green, fuchsia, aqua, yellow, speckled pink, medium bright pink, 2 shades of purple, light and dark orange, and skin tone:** 9˝ squares *each* for fish, seaweed, sea horses, mermaid, sun, and moon*

- **Batting:** 24˝ × 27˝ piece

- **Fusible web:** 2 yards

- **Tear-away stabilizer:** ¾ yard

- **Thread:** Gold metallic, dark blue, purple, white, and green for satin stitch; medium blue for satin stitch and quilting, and invisible thread for quilting

- **Chalk pencil**

- **Painter's Ultra-fine Pen:** Gold metallic

- **Pigma pens:** Red and black

- **Sequins:** 10 round in various colors, 2 gold shell-shaped

- **Seed beads:** 11 dark blue

- **Nonstick (Teflon) pressing sheet**

*If the skin tone fabric is too light for the dark background, double the fabric to prevent shadow through.

CUTTING

Cut all strips across the width of the fabric (selvage to selvage).

- **From the navy:**

  Cut 2 pieces 24˝ × 27˝.*

  Cut 3 strips 2˝ × 40˝.

* One piece is for the appliqué background and is cut oversized; you will trim it after the appliqué is complete.

MAKING SEA GODDESS

Refer to the photos throughout the project for inspiration and ideas for embellishment. The full-sized pattern for *Sea Goddess* is on pullout 2 at the back of the book.

1. Center and transfer the full-sized *Sea Goddess* pattern to one 24˝ × 27˝ rectangle of navy fabric. A chalk pencil and a lightbox help with this step.

Detail of mermaid

2. Prepare the templates for cutting the appliqués. Cut out all the appliqué shapes.

3. Back the entire quilt top with tear-away stabilizer. Position and pin or baste all the appliqué shapes to the marked navy blue piece. Layer the waves first, and then the seaweed, the seahorses, the fish, the mermaid, the sun, and the moon. Fuse all the pieces in place.

Use a nonstick pressing sheet on top of the pattern to layer each fish, the sun, the moon, and the mermaid before placing each entire figure on the background to be fused.

4. Use a satin stitch and the various colored threads to appliqué the shapes in place. Begin by satin stitching the interior of each shape and the edges of the waves before finishing the outside raw edges of each shape. Remove the tear-away stabilizer.

5. Use the gold metallic, red, and black pens to add details such as facial features on the moon and sun, mermaid scales, and additional details on the fish and seahorse bodies. Heat set the markings with a dry iron.

6. Anchor a round sequin with a dark blue bead to create an eye for each fish and seahorse. Add the 2 shell-shaped sequins and the remaining dark blue bead to the mermaid.

7. Trim the appliquéd piece to 19½″ × 22½″.

Use a quilter's ruler and a chalk pencil to mark the trimming lines to be sure the edges are straight and the corners square.

FINISHING THE QUILT

1. Layer the quilt top, batting, and backing. Pin or thread baste the layers together.

2. Use invisible thread to outline quilt each shape. Use medium blue thread to free-motion quilt the ripples in the waves and loops and stars in the sky.

3. Trim and square the quilt to 19½″ × 22½″. Use the 2″ × 40″ navy strips to bind the quilt, using your preferred method.

Detail of seahorses and seaweed

Moonlit Creatures

23″ × 32″, machine appliquéd and quilted by Cyndy Lyle Rymer, Danville, CA, 2006. Fabric generously provided by RJR Fabrics.

MATERIALS

Read through Tips and Techniques for Appliqué and Embellishment (page 50) before beginning this or any project. Refer to that chapter as needed throughout construction. Yardages are based on fabrics with a usable width of 40˝.

- **Dark blue:** 1⅞ yards for background, border triangles, border, binding, and backing

- **Reddish brown:** Fat quarter for background

- **Brown:** ¼ yard for background, coconuts, and palm trees

- **Golden beige:** Fat quarter for cheetahs

- **Lime green:** ¼ yard for palm fronds, leaves, and grasses

- **Gold:** ⅛ yard for background

- **Dark green:** Fat quarter for background, palm fronds, leaves, and grasses

- **Light green, light blue, fuchsia, light purple, yellow, orange, and white:** Scrap of *each* for leaves, flowers, dragonfly, parrots, flowers, moon, and border triangles

- **Batting:** 28˝ × 36˝ piece

- **Fusible web:** 1¼ yards

- **Tear-away stabilizer:** ⅞ yard

- **Thread:** Gold and silver metallic, colors to match fabrics for decorative stitching, and colors to match backgrounds for quilting

- **Fabric paints:** Blue, purple, red, yellow, blue, rust (or sienna), and silver metallic

- **Fabric markers:** Black, gold metallic, blue, light brown, and green

- **Small spray bottle with water**

CUTTING

Cut all strips across the width of the fabric (selvage to selvage).

- **From the dark blue:**

  Cut 1 rectangle 21˝ × 17˝.*

  Cut 2 strips 2½˝ × 40˝.

  Cut 1 rectangle 28˝ × 36˝.

  Cut 4 strips 2˝ × 40˝.

  Cut 2 squares 2⅞˝ × 2⅞˝; cut each square once diagonally to yield 2 half-square triangles (4 total).

- **From the reddish brown:**

  Cut 1 rectangle 21˝ × 14˝.*

- **From the light green, light blue, fuchsia, light purple, yellow, and orange scraps:**

  Cut a *total* of 14 squares, 2⅞˝ × 2⅞˝; cut each square once diagonally to yield 2 half-square triangles (28 total).

* These pieces are cut oversized; you will trim them after the appliqué is complete.

MAKING MOONLIT CREATURES

Refer to the photos throughout the project for inspiration and ideas for embellishment. The full-sized pattern for *Moonlit Creatures* is on pullout 3 at the back of the book.

Painting the Fabric

1. Cover your work surface to protect it for painting.

2. Mix a bit of blue paint with yellow paint to make light green. Refer to the photo below and paint a scrap of yellow fabric for the middle parrot's wings and the top of its head.

Detail of parrots

3. Mix a bit of yellow paint with red paint to make light orange. Paint a white or other light fabric scrap to use for the head of the third parrot. Use the blue and purple paint to shade a scrap of light blue fabric for the body. Paint the tips of the tail and the right wing orange.

4. Use the remaining light orange paint to lightly paint a small scrap of fuchsia fabric for the left wing of the parrot on the left.

5. Trace the cheetah body shapes on the golden beige fabric. Use a small spray bottle to lightly spray the fabric with water. Using the tip of a paintbrush or pencil eraser, paint small dots on the cheetahs' bodies.

6. Trace the moon shape on a white piece of fabric. Paint the fabric with silver metallic paint. Allow all the painted pieces to dry thoroughly.

Assembling the Quilt Top

1. Prepare the templates for cutting the appliqués, including the background shapes. Cut out all the appliqué shapes. Cut the head of the cheetah on the right as a separate piece.

Use small, sharp-tipped scissors to create the desired number of V shapes in the palm fronds.

Detail of palm fronds

2. Fuse the cheetahs' eyes to their faces. Lightly trace the details on the cheetahs' faces with a pencil, and then use the brown fabric marker to add the facial details.

3. Use the green fabric marker to add center veins to the light green palm fronds. You will add the details later with quilting.

4. To create the background, stitch the 21″ × 14″ reddish brown strip to the 21″ × 17″ dark blue rectangle. Referring to the background assembly diagram below, use narrow pieces of fusible web to fuse the brown, gold, and dark green background pieces to the larger reddish brown rectangle.

Background assembly diagram

5. Back the quilt top with tear-away stabilizer. Use matching-colored thread to satin stitch along the upper edge of the reddish brown background piece and the top edge of the dark brown piece.

6. Transfer the full-sized *Moonlit Creatures* pattern to the assembled background.

7. Position and pin or baste the cheetahs, palm tree trunks, palm fronds, and leaves to the marked background piece. Notice that the head of the cheetah on the right overlaps the left palm tree trunk. Position and pin or baste the grasses and leaves. Note that some of the grasses and leaves are overlapped by other appliqué shapes. Fuse all the pieces in place.

8. Using a satin stitch and matching thread, appliqué the cheetahs, palm tree trunks, and some of the larger leaves. Use a straight stitch on the narrower shapes.

9. Position and pin or baste the parrots and flowers. Fuse all the pieces in place.

10. Position and pin or baste the coconuts and dragonfly. Fuse all the pieces in place. Use gold metallic thread to satin stitch around the parrots and dragonfly. Satin stitch the edges of the gold and green background pieces where they are not overlapped by appliqués.

11. Use the black fabric marker to add eye details to the cheetahs. Use gold metallic and blue fabric markers to add the parrots' eyes, details on the center parrot, and details on the dragonfly. Use fabric markers to add the center circles on the flowers.

12. Heat set the paints and inks according to the manufacturer's instructions.

13. Trim the quilt to 19″ by 28″.

14. Sew the dark blue and assorted half-square triangles together in pairs along the long diagonal edges. Press. Make 16.

15. Cut the 2½"-wide blue strips to the lengths shown in the border assembly diagram. Assemble the borders as shown. Press. Add the top and bottom borders, followed by the side borders. Press the seams away from the pieced borders.

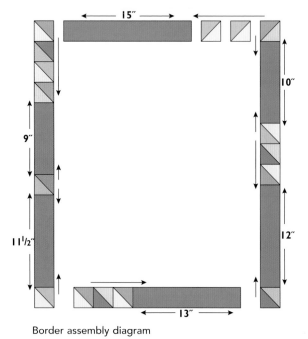

Border assembly diagram

16. Position and fuse the moon so it overlaps the top border. Finish the edges of the moon with a satin stitch in silver metallic thread.

17. Remove the tear-away stabilizer.

FINISHING THE QUILT

1. Layer the quilt top, batting, and backing. Pin or thread baste the layers together.

2. Quilt in-the-ditch around all the major shapes and between the border strips and half-square triangles. Echo quilt around the palm fronds using thread to match the background.

3. Trim and square the quilt as necessary. Use the 2"-wide dark blue strips to bind the quilt, using your preferred method.

Swan Goddess

33¹⁄₄″ × 27¹⁄₄″, machine appliquéd and quilted by Cyndy Lyle Rymer, Danville, CA, 2001.

MATERIALS

Read through Tips and Techniques for Appliqué and Embellishment (page 50) before beginning this or any project. Refer to that chapter as needed throughout construction. Yardages are based on fabrics with a usable width of 40".

- **Light green:** ¾ yard for background
- **Medium green leaf or tone-on-tone print:** 1¾ yards for outer border, backing, and binding
- **Pinkish peach:** ⅝ yard for woman's body
- **White tone-on-tone prints:** Fat quarter *each* of 2 different fabrics for swans
- **Fuchsia:** ¼ yard for inner border and flower parts
- **Assorted greens, yellows, fuchsias, pinks, purples, and blues:** Scraps of *each* for lips, flowers, and leaves
- **Batting:** 37" × 31" piece
- **Fusible web:** 1¼ yards
- **Tear-away stabilizer:** 1½ yards
- **Thread:** Gold metallic and colors to match fabrics for decorative stitching and quilting
- **Fabric paints:** Orange, yellow, white, and blue
- **Fabric markers:** Blue and black

Detail of woman's and swan's faces

CUTTING

Cut all strips across the width of the fabric (selvage to selvage).

- **From the light green:**

  Cut 1 rectangle 29" × 21".

- **From the medium green:**

  Cut 1 rectangle 37" × 31".

  Cut 4 strips 4" × 27¼".

  Cut 4 strips 2" × 40".

- **From the fuchsia:**

  Cut 2 strips 1" × 27¼".

  Cut 2 strips 1" × 20¼".

MAKING SWAN GODDESS

Refer to the photos throughout the project for inspiration and ideas for embellishment. The full-sized pattern for *Swan Goddess* is on pullout 3 at the back of the book.

1. Prepare the templates for cutting the appliqués. Cut out all the appliqué shapes.

2. Cover your work surface to protect it for painting.

3. Use the white fabric paint to paint the white of the eye on the woman's face. Let the paint dry thoroughly. Use the blue fabric marker to add the iris and the black fabric marker to outline the iris. Mix a bit of the white and blue paint to make lavender, and use it as "eye shadow" on the upper and lower lids.

4. Referring to the quilt photo on page 47 and the full-sized pattern for placement, position and fuse the lips to the woman's face.

5. Use the orange fabric paint to paint the tops of the swans' heads. Use the yellow fabric paint to paint the beaks.

6. Heat set the paints and inks according to the manufacturer's instructions.

7. The flower and leaf combinations are made separately and embroidered before being fused to the background. Pin or thread baste a piece of tear-away stabilizer to the back of each piece. Satin stitch the raw edges of the interior portions of each flower or leaf shape using matching threads. You will add the details later with quilting. Remove the stabilizer from the back of each appliqué shape.

8. Center and transfer the full-sized *Swan Goddess* pattern to the 29″ × 21″ light green rectangle.

9. Back the entire quilt top with tear-away stabilizer. Position and pin or baste the prepared flowers and leaves, body, and swan bodies and wings in place. Add the leaves and flowers along the edge of the quilt center. Fuse all the pieces.

10. Use gold metallic thread to satin stitch around the swans and some of the flower parts. Use matching thread to satin stitch around all the flowers and leaves. Remove the tear-away stabilizer.

11. Trim the quilt to 27¼″ × 20¼″.

12. The narrow inner border is sewn into the outer border seam and is unstitched on the inside edge where it overlaps the appliqués. With the wrong sides together, fold the 1″ × 27¼″ fuchsia inner border strips in half lengthwise. Press. Align the raw edges of the top and bottom border strips with the raw edges of the quilt center. Baste ⅛″ from the edge. Repeat to fold, press, and baste the 1″ × 20¼″ inner border strips to the sides.

13. Add the top and bottom outer borders and then the side borders using a ¼″ seam allowance. The inner borders are secured as the outer borders are sewn. Press the outer border seams toward the quilt center.

FINISHING THE QUILT

1. Layer the quilt top, batting, and backing. Pin or thread baste the layers together.

2. Using light green thread to match the background, quilt in-the-ditch around all the major shapes. Free-motion quilt the details in the wings with white thread. Outline quilt the leaf shapes in the outer border print, if applicable, with matching thread.

3. Trim and square the quilt as necessary. Use the 2″ × 40″ medium green strips to bind the quilt, using your preferred method.

Home, Sweet Home

Instead of binding this quilt, do as Cyndy did: cut the outer borders a few inches wider—for example, 6″ wide–and then cut the batting and backing larger to accommodate the larger quilt size. Rather than binding the quilt as described in Finishing the Quilt, Step 3 above, stretch the quilt over an appropriately sized wooden frame or stretcher bars, and staple or tack the quilt into a picture frame.

Detail of flowers and leaves

Tips and Techniques for Appliqué and Embellishment

Read through the following instructions carefully before you begin a project, and return to these pages as needed as you work. In addition, read through the complete project instructions before you begin any specific project.

SUGGESTED FABRICS AND BATTING

The projects in this book were made with 100% cotton fabrics. These fabrics are widely available, and most people will find them the easiest to work with. Recommended cottons include batiks, marbled and hand-dyed fabrics, small abstract prints, geometric prints, and solids.

Various thin battings, including cotton, polyester, and poly/cotton blend, were used for the different projects in the book.

Fabrics like these make great choices for the quilts in this book.

PREPARING FOR APPLIQUÉ

The pullouts at the back of the book include full-sized patterns for *Earth Mother* (page 16), *Kindred Spirits of the Jungle* (page 34), *Sea Goddess* (page 38), *Moonlit Creatures* (page 42), and *Swan Goddess* (page 47). Patterns for *Pajaros* (page 8), *Celestial Birds* (page 12), *Folkloric Fish* (page 20), and the *Spirits of the Sky* table runner (page 28) will need to be enlarged before you begin. A photocopy center will enlarge these patterns to the percentages suggested on the pattern pages. In some cases, you may need to enlarge the patterns in a two-step process; this may cost a little more. Note that while the patterns give you the enlargement percentages you'll need to create the projects as shown, you can make your project larger or smaller simply by adjusting the enlargement percentage.

The majority of the projects in this book were made using machine appliqué techniques. However, if you prefer, you can use traditional needle-turn appliqué techniques for most projects instead. *Pajaros* (page 8) was completed in this manner. Simply add $\frac{1}{8}''$ to $\frac{3}{16}''$ turn-under allowances around all pattern pieces.

Preparing the Background Fabric

To help place the appliqué pieces on your background fabric, trace the black lines on the patterns onto the background fabric using a mechanical pencil, a white or silver pencil, or a fine-point permanent pen. A lightbox or a bright window is useful for this step and works whether you are using a light or a dark background fabric.

If you are using a light background fabric, you should be able to see the major outlines without the aid of a lightbox or window. Simply place the background fabric directly over the pattern and position the fabric pieces as you work.

Transfer the pattern to the background fabric.

Study the pattern to determine how you will layer the pieces. You may find it helpful to make a photocopy of the pattern and jot down notes about the layering order. While you will generally want to work from the bottom layer to the top layer, there will be exceptions; for example, it is best to overlap dark-colored pieces over lighter pieces to avoid "shadow through" from the dark pieces underneath. As you cut out the fabric pieces, mark any areas that will be overlapped by other pieces.

tip

If you like to plan ahead, create a "fabric key" to help you remember where you plan to use your different fabrics. Tape small scraps of fabric for each piece to a copy of the pattern.

Create a fabric key to help with fabric placement.

Preparing the Appliqué Shapes

Use a fine-point permanent pen to trace the individual pattern pieces from the master pattern to the rough (webbed) side of a lightweight paper-backed fusible web. (If you prefer drawing on the paper side of the fusible web, you will need to reverse the drawing. Take the pattern to a photocopy center to have it reversed.) Add at least a ¼″ allowance to any area on an appliqué piece that will be overlapped by another piece.

Add a minimum ¼″ to areas that will be overlapped by another appliqué shape.

To avoid bulk and stiffness in larger pieces, you can cut away the inside area of the fusible web, leaving a ½″ outline. Use the cutaway interfacing for smaller shapes.

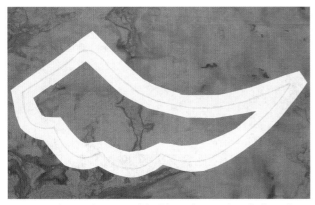

Cut away the inside areas of fusible web to reduce bulk and stiffness in large appliqué shapes.

Follow the manufacturer's instructions to fuse the shape, web side down, to the wrong side of the appropriate appliqué fabric. Mark the edges that will be overlapped. You can either fuse all the pieces at once, filling in any gaps as needed, or you can fuse and stitch as you go. Note that in some places where shapes extend into borders, you will need to keep the paper backing on, pin part of the shape out of the way, and finish fusing after the entire quilt top has been sewn together.

tip

Use a nonstick pressing cloth to keep your iron and pressing surface clean. If you *do* get fusible web on your iron, clean the iron with iron cleaner before you continue. You don't want to get the adhesive on the rest of your work!

Thick gray lines on all patterns indicate details to add with decorative stitching, paint, or other embellishments. To make embellishment easier, mark the desired details on the fabric with a pencil or fine-point permanent pen. Use a lightbox for tracing if necessary, or—as an alternative for tracing small areas—make your own lightbox with a piece of glass or Plexiglas and a light source (e.g., lamp or flashlight) underneath. You can also use a Plexiglas quilting extension if you have one for your sewing machine. For another easy solution, tape the original pattern to a large window, then tape the base layer over the pattern and trace.

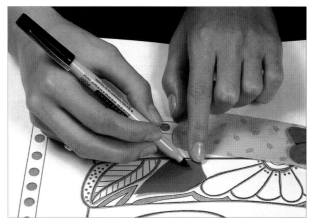

Mark the pieces for decorative stitching, painting, or other embellishment.

STITCHING

Interpreting Laurel's artwork in fabric offers you the opportunity to play with all the decorative stitches your machine has to offer. You can even create new stitches if you own an embroidery machine and the necessary embroidery software. As always, experiment first on a scrap before stitching on your project. Use a stabilizer under your stitching to prevent the "molehills" and "tunneling" that can form when you are doing satin stitching and other heavy stitching. You can use cutaway stabilizer, tearaway stabilizer, or freezer paper. Be sure to remove the stabilizer after you complete the stitching.

Where there are multiple layers of fabric, it's often best to do the decorative stitching on individual pieces before adding them to the background layer. For example, satin stitching can be added around facial features before the entire face is fused to the background.

After stitching all the layered pieces, cut away the fabric underneath, leaving a ¼″ seam allowance to prevent fabric buildup. Try not to have more than two layers of fabric on top of each other.

Selecting Threads and Needles

Besides working with a variety of stitches, you can also play with many different types of thread. Just about any type of thread works for embellishment: cotton in various weights, embroidery floss, perle cotton, metallics, and rayons. Use cotton or silk thread for hand appliqué. For machine stitching, in addition to cotton, we recommend rayon and metallic threads to give these projects texture and sparkle. The threads we used most often were 40-weight rayon and metallic varieties. You'll find some specific recommendations as you read about the various stitching techniques in the next few pages.

Use needles that are suitable for the technique and the thread that you plan to use:

- Embroidery/rayon thread: use a needle designed for embroidery or rayon thread

- Metallic thread: use a needle designed for metallic thread

- Nylon thread: use a needle of appropriate size for the thread weight

- Hand quilting: use a betweens, ranging in size from 8 (longer) to 12 (shorter)

- Hand appliqué: use a #11 sharp or #11 milliner's needle

- Machine quilting: use a quilting or jeans needle

Don't limit your embellishments to paint and thread. You can stitch or use fabric glue to attach beads, sequins, buttons, shells, or any other type of embellishment to add extra detail, texture, and visual excitement to your piece.

Use a thread type and needle that are appropriate for the stitching you intend to do and have fun with beads, buttons, sequins, and trims.

The Satin Stitch

The satin stitch is an excellent choice for machine appliqué. Good satin stitching takes time and practice. Relax, put on some good music, and have fun. Here are some tips to keep in mind to improve your enjoyment—and the outcome—of your satin-stitching experience.

- If you haven't done much satin stitching, practice on some samples first—you may need to adjust the tension on your sewing machine.

- Some stitchers use a lightweight bobbin thread, which doesn't add additional bulk to the back of the design. Loosen the tension as needed to make sure the bobbin thread doesn't show on the top. Bobbin thread is usually sold on larger spools or on prewound bobbins, and is most widely available in black and white.

- Use an open-toe appliqué foot (shown in the photos on pages 55–56) so you can see exactly where you're stitching.

- Set the stitch on your machine so it is wide enough to cover the raw edges of the fabric shapes and so that the stitch density is to your liking. Too many stitches will make the fabric pucker, causing molehills, while too few stitches will give an uneven look.

- Experiment with different stitch widths for variety. Try tapering or widening the stitches as you go—for example, tapering to the points of leaves or widening for decorative wedges.

Detail of *Kindred Spirits of the Jungle*

Starting and Stopping

Start by securing your stitches. Some stitchers pull the threads to the top, knot them, stitch over the tails for a bit, and then clip the loose thread tails (see photo below). You can also take several tiny stitches in place, then adjust the stitch to the desired setting and proceed. To end a line of stitching, pull the thread to the back, knot it, and carefully trim the tails close to the surface.

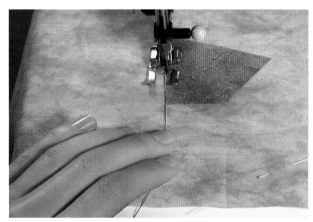

Pull the starting stitches to the top, knot them, and stitch over the tails to secure.

Pivoting

Use the needle-down position for stopping and pivoting to negotiate tight curves, as well as to turn corners. Think about where you want the next stitch to be when you start stitching and leave the needle in the position that will allow you to do that.

For example, for a corner or curve, stop with the needle down on the outside edge of the stitch, lift the presser foot, and turn the fabric. When you start stitching again, the needle will be on the outside edge of the new line of stitching. This allows you to stitch over the end of the previous stitching, giving you a clean corner or curve.

You'll get a smoother curve if you make a number of small pivots rather than just one or two larger pivots as you turn.

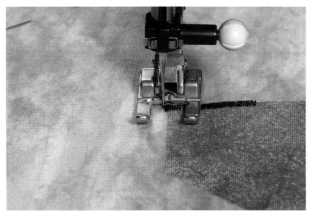

Pivoting for an inside corner or curve

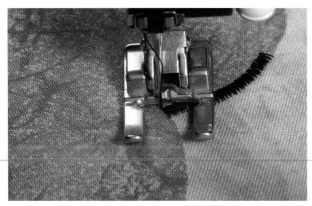

Pivoting for an outside corner or curve

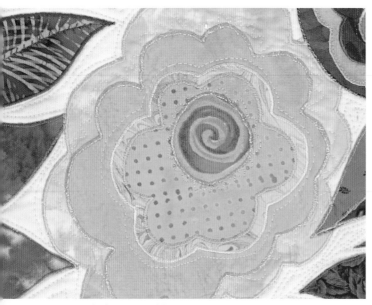

Detail of *Swan Goddess*

Other Decorative Stitches

If you have a machine that does embroidery, this is a great opportunity to use a variety of stitches, especially geometrics—circles, triangles, wedges, or squares. If you are ambitious and have an embroidery machine and software, you can design your own stitches to use in your project.

Example of decorative stitching

Effectively add decorative outlines and various details, such as leaf veins, with straight stitching. A heavier-weight cotton or metallic thread shows best.

Example of straight stitching for detail

Machine Quilting

Use either 100% cotton (regular or topstitch) or invisible monofilament thread (nylon or polyester) to outline quilt the major shapes or pieces and to hold everything in place. Add other decorative quilting as desired. Quilting on most projects in this book was kept to a minimum so as not to compete with the appliquéd and embellished designs.

PAINTING, STAMPING, AND OTHER CREATIVE DELIGHTS

Whatever method you use to add painted, stamped, or drawn details, be sure to follow the manufacturer's instructions for product use, and practice on a scrap of fabric first. See Resources and Bibliography on page 61 for product information.

Painting

You have two options for when to add paint embellishment:

- You can add stamped, painted, and drawn details to shapes before you cut them out and fuse them to the quilt top. With this method, you don't need to worry about making mistakes on the assembled quilt top. You can also embellish a larger piece of fabric than you need so you can select the area of the embellished fabric you like the best.

- You can add details after all the shapes have been fused. You might want to use this approach when adding smaller details to the background, such as in *Earth Mother* (page 16).

Detail of *Earth Mother*

If you are uncomfortable painting or drawing free-hand, place the paper pattern on a lightbox (or makeshift lightbox) and place the fabric directly over the pattern. You will be able to see and trace the shapes by following the lines on the pattern. This will work for all but the very darkest background fabrics.

Fine-point brushes are great for creating lines, spirals, small dots, and other decorative shapes. Use a plate or other washable flat surface for a palette. For quick cleanup, you can't beat a coated paper plate.

If you want to add a thin layer of a color for texture or depth, or want to transition from one color to another, try sponging. Use a piece of sea sponge and opaque fabric paints such as those listed on page 58. Gently sponge on the color with a light touch. As with the other painting techniques, use a plate or washable flat surface as a palette. Blot the sponge before applying the paint to fabric, and practice on scraps until you get the effect you want.

Sponging can add color, texture, and depth to your fabric.

Use opaque paints to paint a light color on a dark piece of fabric. It also helps to paint the shape with an opaque white first, let it dry, and then paint the final color over the white.

Stamping

A huge variety of stamps are available for purchase in shops, via mail order, and over the Internet. Just be sure you purchase fabric stamps and not stamps made for paper. There are several types of stamps to try: sponge stamps, foam stamps, and harder rubber stamps. Each gives a different result, so experiment to see which type you like best for your project.

Experiment to see which type of stamp gives you the desired results.

If you wish, you can make your own stamps from sheets of art foam or from erasers. A pencil eraser is great for dots; use a fatter pencil for larger dots.

Use the eraser end of a fat pencil to stamp dots on fabric.

Types of Paint to Use

It's best to use fabric paints that can be ironed. Some "puff" paints will melt and stick to your iron. If you use puff paints, apply them as the last step, after all the fusing and pressing is done. Allow all paints to dry thoroughly and—with the exception of puff paints—heat them according to the manufacturer's instructions. Some paints come in a bottle with an applicator tip that allows you to apply the paint directly from the bottle. See Resources and Bibliography on page 61 for information on where to find the various paint products.

Use paints specifically designed for fabrics.

Types of paints used for the projects in this book include the following:

Acclaim Fabri-Tex (a textile medium that can be added to make any water-based paint suitable for use on fabric; it adds flexibility to dry painted surfaces and makes the paint more permanent when heat set)

Fabric Paints by Plaid (available in translucent, metallic, and sparkle/glitter)

Jacquard Traditional Paints (available in translucent, opaque, and metallic)

Lumiere Fabric Paints (metallic)

Neopaque Fabric Paints (opaque)

Setacolor Fabric Paints (available in translucent, opaque, and pearlescent)

Versatex Textile Paints (available in translucent, opaque, pearlescent, and metallic)

tips *and tricks*
for fabric stamping

1. Stamps without a lot of intricate detail work best for stamping paint on fabric.

2. Pad your work surface to get a good stamped image.

3. Apply a thin coat of paint to the stamp with a small foam paintbrush.

4. Stamp the image firmly on the fabric using a straight "down and up" motion.

5. Heat set the paint following the manufacturer's instructions.

6. Always clean your stamps after using them. Hold them under running water and scrub them with a fingernail brush or old toothbrush.

Colored and Metallic Permanent Pens

Permanent pens can be used to add details or for drawing decorative shapes. These pens are also great for outlining. Practice on a scrap of fabric to make sure the ink doesn't spread or bleed.

tip

You can color white areas of black-and-white fabrics—especially geometrics—with paints, fabric pens, crayons, or colored pencils to create just the right effect.

Enhance black-and-white fabrics with fabric crayons, pencils, or markers.

Resources and Bibliography

Sources and Information for Products Referenced

For art or sewing supplies, check your local quilting, sewing, or art/craft store. In addition, you can explore the following resources:

For fast2fuse and other quilting supplies:

The Cotton Patch
3405 Hall Lane, Dept. CTB
Lafayette, CA 94549
(800) 835-4418
(925) 283-7883
www.quiltusa.com

Keepsake Quilting
P.O. Box 1618
Center Harbor, NH 03226
(800) 865-9458
www.keepsakequilting.com

For "exotic" fabrics and embellishments:

St. Theresa Textile Trove
1329 Main Street
Cincinnati, OH 45202
(800) 236-2450
www.sttheresatextile.com

For fabric paints and supplies:

Dharma Trading Company
1604 Fourth Street
San Rafael, CA 94901
(800) 542-5227
(415) 456-1211
www.dharmatrading.com

For fabric stamps and paints:

Hot Potatoes
2805 Columbine Place
Nashville, TN 37204
(615) 269-8002
www.hotpotatoes.com

For beads and beading supplies:

TWE/BEADS
P. O. Box 55
Hamburg, NJ 07419
(973) 209-1517
www.twebeads.com

For Quilting Paper and other quilting notions:

Golden Threads
2 S. 373 Seneca Drive
Wheaton, IL 60187
(888) 477-7718
(630) 231-2800
www.goldenthreads.com

For information about batting and Steam-A-Seam fusibles:

The Warm Company
954 E. Union Street
Seattle, WA 98122
(800) 234-WARM
(206) 320-9276
www.warmcompany.com

For information about thread:

Superior Threads
P.O. Box 1672
St. George, UT 84771
(800) 499-1777
www.superiorthreads.com

Robison-Anton Textile Company
P.O. Box 159
Fairview, NJ 07022
(201) 941-0500
www.robison-anton.com

For information about thread and stabilizers:

Sulky of America
P.O. Box 494129
Port Charlotte, FL 33949
(800) 874-4115
info@sulky.com
www.sulky.com

For Laurel Burch embroidery designs:

Oklahoma Embroidery Supply & Design
www.embroideryonline.com

Recommended Reading

Anderson, Alex. *Start Quilting* (2nd edition), C&T Publishing: Lafayette, CA, 2004.

Hargrave, Harriet, *Heirloom Machine Quilting* (4th edition), C&T Publishing: Lafayette, CA, 2004.

_____. *Mastering Machine Appliqué*, C&T Publishing: Lafayette, CA, 1991.

Hargrave, Harriet and Sharyn Craig. *The Art of Classic Quiltmaking*, C&T Publishing: Lafayette, CA, 2000.

Sandbach, Kathy. *Show Me How to Machine Quilt*, C&T Publishing: Lafayette, CA, 2002.

Stori, Mary. *Beading Basics*, C&T Publishing: Lafayette, CA, 2004.

Wasilowski, Laura. *Fusing Fun!* C&T Publishing: Lafayette, CA, 2005.

Wells, Jean. *Machine Appliqué Made Easy*, C&T Publishing: Lafayette, CA, 2005.

Wells, Jean and Valori Wells. *Pillows: 29 Projects for Stylish Living*, C&T Publishing: Lafayette, CA, 2006.

Meet Laurel

Laurel Burch began making jewelry in the Haight-Ashbury area of San Francisco in the late 1960s, selling her designs on the street and in local galleries. Today, Laurel is an internationally renowned artist and designer with a flourishing business based in Marin County, California.

Great Titles
from  C&T PUBLISHING